THE PROMISE OF THE HOLY SPIRIT.

Sermon No. 2

W. W. PRESCOTT.

1893
GENERAL CONFERENCE BULLETTIN

Published by
The Return of the Latter Rain Publishers
1--866-546-6469

PREFACE

Now I want to show you that it is the mercy of God that this special outpouring of his Spirit does not come upon those who are cherishing sin. I want you to note that point when praying for the outpouring of the Spirit, and I want you to see that it is the special mercy of God that he does not directly answer these prayers to any one of us who are cherishing sins....Everyone who asks for this and is cherishing known sins, is asking for his own destruction, as Ananias and Sapphira were destroyed. It is the great long-suffering of God that such prayers are not immediately answered, and He waits that they may be answered without destroying us.

W.W. Prescott, pages 64-65

THE PROMISE OF THE HOLY SPIRIT. --- No. 2.

W. W. PRESCOTT.

HEB.1:9: "Thou hast loved righteousness, and hated iniquity: therefore God, even thy God, hath anointed thee with the oil of gladness above thy fellows." This scripture of course refers to Christ, and we wish to note one or two things about it before we take the general meaning. "Thou hast loved righteousness, and hated iniquity." This word iniquity [63] is the same word that is in 1 John 3:4,—transgression of the law—"Whosoever committeth sin transgresseth also the law; for sin is the transgression of the law," or iniquity, or lawlessness. Thou hast loved righteousness, and hated the transgression of the law, or hated lawlessness; "therefore God, even thy God, hath anointed thee with the oil of gladness above thy fellows." Fellows. This word "fellows" is found in the seventh verse of the fifth chapter of Luke where it is translated partners. "And they beckoned unto their partners, which were in the other ship." Their partners. Now I will read the verse a little different. Thou hast loved righteousness and hated sin, iniquity, transgression of the law, "therefore God, even thy God, hath anointed thee with the oil of gladness above thy partners." Who are the partners? Why, we are the partners; we are workers together with God, we are laborers together with him, we are God's fellow-workers.

Now turn if you please, to Acts 10:37, 38: "That word, I say ye know, which was published throughout all Judea, and began from Galilee, after the baptism which John preached; how God anointed Jesus of Nazareth with the Holy Ghost and with power: who went about doing good, and healing all that were oppressed of the devil; for God was with him." You will remember the testimony that was borne about Jesus by Nicodemus, as recorded in the third chapter of John and the second verse. "For no man can do these miracles that thou doest, except God be with him." Read in Mark 16:17, 18: "And these signs shall follow them that believe: in my name shall they cast out devils; they shall speak with new tongues; they shall take up serpents; and if they drink any deadly thing, it shall not hurt them; they shall lay hands on the sick, and they shall recover."

Now it is said of Christ, "How God anointed Jesus of Nazareth with the Holy Ghost, and with power: who went about doing good, and healing all that were oppressed of the devil; for God was with him." This is the anointing spoken of in the first text. "God hath anointed thee with the oil of gladness above thy fellows." It is very easy to see without taking any length of time to explain it, why this is spoken of in this way. That anointing oil with which it is called the oil of gladness, we learn from Rom.14:17, "For the kingdom of God is not meat and drink; but righteousness, and peace, and joy in the Holy Ghost." So it is called anointing with the oil of gladness.

But the objective point that I want to note is the reason why he was anointed with the "oil of gladness," above others, his partners, his fellow workers, his fellow laborers. The reason is because he loved righteousness and hated sin, hated iniquity, and hated everything different from God. That was the reason. He loved righteousness and hated sin, hated iniquity. And hating iniquity, as it is spoken of in this text, means more than a mere passing dislike for it, feeling a little uncomfortable under it. A perfect hatred for sin! And in this very fact is seen a wondrous trait in the character of Christ. So in the work that he did for us here, although he hated sin with a perfect hatred, hated, yet he gathered to himself all the results of sin; put himself right in the place of the sinner, to bear the results of every sin; and not simply that way, but he took those things right to his very soul; and he endured, in taking upon himself the consequences of sin, what we cannot possibly comprehend, because we cannot understand the perfect hatred with which he regarded sin.

The fact is, our minds have become blunted and dull, and we have become accustomed to sin, and sin has left its impression upon our minds.

Sin is a perfect horror of blackness; sin is the horror of great darkness, and yet we have become so accustomed to it that it makes little impression upon our minds. We cannot understand, we cannot appreciate the feeling with which Christ regarded sin. Sin is being contrary to God. Now when Christ, who had been one with the Father, one in every thought and purpose, in every work, thus voluntarily put himself in that attitude where he must suffer the consequences of sin, put himself in the place of those who were out of harmony with God, he voluntarily put himself out of harmony with God, by taking this sin; although he hated iniquity and loved righteousness, he came to this world, put himself right in the sinner's place for our sakes; (and we cannot begin to appreciate what this meant to him) --- all this was done that we may appreciate how God looks upon sin.

Sin is not simply doing a thing; it is being in that condition. Sin in the character, is being out of harmony with God, is being different from God. Now, Christ voluntarily put himself there, although there was that perfect union between him and the Father, and since that perfect union was the same in thoughts, purposes, and plans, yet he put himself where of necessity God must treat him as though he was out of harmony with him; and it was that experience that brought out that cry of anguish: "My God, my God, why hast thou forsaken me?" But for this experience here upon earth, because he loved righteousness and hated iniquity, God anointed him with the oil of gladness above his fellows, or above his partners.

The same idea is expressed in different words in John 3:34: "For he whom God hath sent speaketh the words of God: for God giveth not the spirit by [64] measure unto him." A bountiful pouring out of it, no measure at all, a perfect, bountiful pouring out of it and anointing above his fellows. Why? Because he loved righteousness and hated iniquity; because he spoke the words of God. That is why God dealt with him in that way. So in John 6:27, we have the expression "Labor not for the meat which perisheth, but for that meat which endureth unto everlasting life, which the Son of man shall give unto you: for him hath God the Father sealed." God anointed him with the oil of gladness," — a simple figure of expression for the giving of the Spirit to him, and the figure of anointing the priests with the oil. He gave the spirit to him by no measure, because he spoke the words of God, because God dwelt in him, and he yielded himself to God that He himself might appear in him, and that his character might also appear, and so had God the Father sealed him.

Now I do not intend to undertake to take up at any length the idea of what it is to be sealed, but just refer to two or three scriptures, and leave that subject till later. Eph.1:13, and also 4:30, "And grieve not the Holy Spirit of God, whereby ye are sealed unto the day of redemption." 2Cor.1:22, "Who hath also sealed us, and given the earnest of the Spirit in our hearts." It is evidently in connection with this sealing work, and we read some scriptures last night in regard to this sealing, receiving the seal of God in the forehead, and the number that was sealed, and how that the four winds were held while this sealing work was going on, that the Holy Spirit must appear in this way, and that it is that by which we are sealed to the day of redemption. So God sealed his Son by giving to him the Holy Spirit. Now, the Holy Spirit is given in a greater or less degree to every one because it is the agency through which God works and draws us to himself, to work with us in this way.

But you understand that our study just now is upon the special outpouring of the Spirit; more than the ordinary outpouring of the Spirit - the special outpouring of the Spirit, and the task to which we have applied ourselves, is to find out what hinders it, and so remove it. Not that the Spirit of God has not been given in any degree to his people, here and elsewhere, for which we are all thankful, but it is time for more than the ordinary display of his power, it is time for the special outpouring. Now, we want to know what hinders its taking place immediately. Now we want to know what hinders that it does not take place right here. In the first text that I read, we find, because "Thou hast loved righteousness and hated iniquity." That is why God gave Christ the Spirit without measure, and I say that the presence of sin and the practice of iniquity is what hinders it.

Now I want to show you that it is the mercy of God that this special outpouring of his Spirit does not come upon those who are cherishing sin. I want you to note that point when praying for the outpouring of the Spirit, and I want you to see that it is the special mercy of God that he does not directly answer these prayers to any one of us who are cherishing sins. In the twelfth chapter of Heb., and the twenty-ninth verse, the statement is made, "For our God is a consuming fire," and you remember in the record of Ex.19 when God came down upon Mt. Sinai, the strict commands concerning the people's approaching near the mount, and we read in verse 18, "And mount Sinai was altogether on a smoke, because the Lord descended upon it in fire: and the smoke thereof ascended as the smoke of a furnace and the whole mount quaked greatly."

In Ex.24:17, we read "And the sight of the glory of the Lord was like devouring fire on the top of the mount in the eyes of the children of Israel," and you remember how the people were frightened, and the explicit commands given them by God that they should not step beyond a certain line, and that they should not come into his immediate presence, and that if they did, they would be destroyed at once. When Moses came down from the mount, the people could not look at his countenance in their sinful condition.

Turning to Acts 2:2-4, we read concerning the special display of the outpouring of the Spirit of God, "And suddenly there came a sound from heaven as of a rushing mighty wind, and it filled all the house where they were sitting, and there appeared unto them cloven tongues like as of fire, and it sat upon each of them. And they were all filled with the Holy Ghost, and began to speak in other tongues, as the Spirit gave them utterance."

Now, what was the experience they had preparatory to that day of Pentecost, before receiving the Holy Spirit? We read in John 20:22, "Receive ye the Holy Ghost." That was several days before this experience. But the day of Pentecost was the time for the special presence of God, and the outpouring of his Spirit. His special power was manifested in the forked flames of fire. Those darting tongues of fire appeared there, and sat upon them. Now those disciples would have been consumed by that very display, and so would you and I, if this same experience came to us with sin about us. I say, it is a very solemn thing in more ways than one to ask God for the special outpouring of his Spirit as on the day of Pentecost. Everyone who asks for this and is cherishing known sins, is asking for his own destruction, as Ananias and Sapphira were destroyed. It is the great long-suffering of God that such prayers are not immediately [65] answered, and He waits that they may be answered without destroying us.

God's purpose is that sin should be destroyed, and his presence, unveiled, destroys sin always and everywhere. Sin cannot come into the presence of God. It is entirely impossible that it should do so; and with whomsoever sin is found in the presence of God, in destroying that sin, the person himself is destroyed, because sin is through and through him; it is his very being, from the crown of his head to the soles of his feet, and throughout. Now it is utterly impossible for us to separate sin from ourselves. God can do that thing; God can take sin from us, but he will not take that from us contrary to our will. When he tells us that that is sin, and that He wants to remove it, we must consent to it, or it will not be removed. When fire and brimstone is called down from heaven, it will be simply the glory of God's presence that will destroy sinners. They cannot stand before him.

Read Isa.33:13-16, and see what experience is necessary in order that we may stand in such circumstances: "Hear, ye that are far off, what I have done; and, ye that are near, acknowledge my might. The sinners in Zion are afraid; fearfulness hath surprised the hypocrites. Who among us shall dwell with the devouring fire? who among us shall dwell with everlasting burnings? He that walketh righteously, and speaketh uprightly; he that despiseth the gain of oppressions, that shaketh his hands from holding of bribes, that stoppeth his ears from hearing of blood, and shutteth his eyes from seeing evil; he shall dwell on high: his place of defense shall be the munitions of rocks; bread shall be given him; his waters shall be sure." Now that experience is necessary.

What was the experience of the disciples as a preparation for this outpouring? Let us read a brief statement concerning it:-

"For ten days the disciples prayed before the Pentecostal blessing came. Then it required all that time to bring them to an understanding of what it meant to offer effectual prayer, drawing nearer and nearer to God, confessing their sins, humbling their hearts before God, and by faith beholding Jesus, and becoming changed into his image." - Special Test., No. 2, p.19.

Now I want you to think of this. Those disciples had been with Christ for three and a half years, had seen him after his resurrection, sat and spoke with him, but had not yet received the Holy Ghost, and even after his ascension, before this special blessing could come upon them, it required ten days of confession and repentance in order not to be consumed by that blessing.

Now, if that was the case with them, what shall we say of ourselves? To my mind, the worst feature of the whole situation is just what the Laodicean message says, and the worst is we don't see it. Now, if we don't see it, let us take the word of God as it is, and say it is so, let us so continue. We have sinned and done iniquity, and there is no good thing in us. Day by day let us draw near to God by repentance and confession, and God will draw near to us with mercy and forgiveness. Now that is the point that I want to dwell specially upon, that the reason why the special outpouring of the Spirit of God does not come upon his people, is that they must repent, else they would be consumed by it. Let me read just a word here to show the relation of repentance and confession and the removal of sin to this outpouring of the Spirit:-

"Not one of us will ever receive the seal of God while our characters have one spot or stain upon them. It is left with us to remedy the defects in our characters, to cleanse the soul-temple of every defilement. Then the latter rain will fall upon us as the early rain fell upon the disciples on the day of Pentecost." - Test. 31, p. 210.

Now, there is the whole matter in a few words; and I say we must face this now. It is no use to let these things slide easily. Now, these things are for me, and these things are for every one here, as the solemn message of God to his soul. Not one of us will ever receive the seal of God while our characters have one spot or stain upon them.

Thou hast anointed him with the oil of gladness above his fellows. Why? - Because he loved righteousness and hated iniquity. "It is left with us to remedy the defects in our characters, to cleanse the soul-temple of every defilement." And there is no question about it. "Then the latter rain will fall upon us as the early rain fell upon the disciples on the day of Pentecost." Now, that is just as simple and plain a statement as can be. What is the thing for us to do? It seems to me, for me personally, and for every one who desires this experience, that it is to begin to confess our sinfulness to God with humility of soul, with deep contrition before God to be zealous and repent. Now, that is the only message that I can bring to-night. It is just that.

Now the question as to whether there is any need of it. Suppose we say we do not see anything to confess at all. That does not touch the matter in any way. When God sends us word that we are sinful, it is for us to say we are so, whether we can see it or not. That should be our experience. We feel rich and increased in goods, and know not that we are wretched and miserable and blind and naked. This is just our condition exactly, whether we can see it or not. When God sends us a message and tells us to believe it, it is time for us to be about it. When he sends out these instructions, it is time that we should confess our sins, and set about to remove them, and to see how long a time it will take, just notice this example in 2Sam.12, where the Lord [66] sent the prophet Nathaniel to David, who said "Thou art the man." In verse 13 we read, "And David said unto Nathan, I have sinned against the Lord. And Nathan said unto David, The Lord hath also put away thy sin; thou shalt not die." Now, that is the length of time that it requires. But, until we come to that point where we can say personally, "I have sinned against the Lord," he will not put away the sin, because, in the order of his plan, he will not remove sin from us contrary to our acknowledgment; all that he asks of us is to acknowledge sin.

Notice this in Jer.3:13: "Only acknowledge thine iniquity, that thou hast transgressed against the Lord thy God." Read also verse 12: "Go and proclaim these words toward the north, and say, Return, thou backsliding Israel, saith the Lord; and I will not cause mine anger to fall upon you: for I am merciful, saith the Lord, and I will not keep anger forever." Simply acknowledge the iniquity, the sin; that is what he asks, and,

15

"If we confess our sins, he is faithful and just to forgive us our sins, and to cleanse us from all unrighteousness."

Now we have come to this time when the light has begun to shine, that is, the light which is to light the earth with its glory; and the angel has descended to unite with the third angel to swell this "loud cry." We found last night that only those would be permitted to take a part in this work during the "loud cry" who have resisted temptation in the strength of the Mighty One; and that is simply another expression for those who have cleansed their souls from defilement; that is, they have repented of their sins, and God has removed them. I don't know what it will take, I am sure, but it seems to me sometimes that there will be something to awaken us to the way that God looks at sin, and the way he looks at us. But we have refused the warning of the Spirit, and the instruction that he has sent, and the testimonies that he has sent us again and again right on this point: "Repent, and do the first works; or else I will come unto thee quickly, and will remove thy candlestick out of his place." For years this has been the warning, repent! repent! repent! But we have not heeded this testimony, but have come to that point where we say: "I am rich and increased with goods, and have need of nothing."

And yet I say that if ever there was a needy company, it is this company.

Now God has made it just as plain as can be, just as plain as that two and two are four, and this instruction is not one that has come to us a long while ago, either. Let me read:-

"I have been shown that impure practices, pride, selfishness, self-glorying have closed the door of the heart, even of those who teach the truth to others, so that the frown of God is upon them. Cannot some renovating power take hold of them? Have they fallen a prey to a moral disease which is incurable because they themselves refused to be cured?"

That is the point; God can cure it, unless we refuse to allow him to take hold of the case. Read further on:-

"O that every one who labors in word and doctrine would heed the words of Paul, 'I beseech you therefore, brethren, by the mercies of God, that ye present your bodies a living sacrifice, holy, acceptable unto God, which is your reasonable service.'"

Again, under an article of the same date:- "We have been asked why there is so little efficiency among our teachers. The answer is that it is because known sin in various forms is cherished among the professed followers of Christ, and the conscience becomes hardened by long violation."

Notice that it is not sins of ignorance. It is because, in spite of all the light that has come to us, all the reproof and instruction, we cherish known sins. I say, we do that and yet are praying for the special outpouring of his Spirit upon us when it would mean death to us. Now, I say it is a solemn thing, and we stand in a solemn place. There is sin cherished among us; there is no question about it. We are cherishing known sins.

Now, we may go on cherishing these known sins, and if God heard our prayers and made this special outpouring of his Spirit as upon the day of Pentecost upon us, it would bring death upon every one who is in that condition. If we go on without that special outpouring and without that Spirit, and still cherish those known sins, the glory of God when he comes would cause our death then, just the same, to say nothing about the second death. Now, if we are ready to die to-night, we may live in Christ Jesus. But those who persist to hold to sin, they shall surely die a little later, and that involves the second death also.

Now I am perfectly aware that I am speaking with great plainness, and I do not speak this without thought and prayer. I speak what I believe to be the message of God to our souls, mine and yours. I say that it is time for us to be zealous and repent that God's special outpouring of his Spirit may come upon us without destroying us. If we don't make this matter a matter of earnest prayer, I say it simply means death to you and to me. And it seems to me, that the laborer who would go out from this Conference without a special experience in the blessing and power of God through repentance and acceptance of Christ, and the special presence of God with him, would as it were, go to his very death then, because the power of Satan is to be manifested in a wonderful manner. We are beginning to see that that is so. Now the only thing that preserves any one who goes out in the glorious cause of truth, is the special power of God manifested in his behalf, t0 [67] keep him physically I mean, from calamity and destruction, because Satan aims to destroy every one who would attempt to enlighten the people at this time.

As we are now just at the close of time, and the light has come to enlighten the world, Satan's purpose is to destroy physically, and cause the death of every messenger of the cause who goes out to give light. And it is just because the angels of God are commissioned to take care of these messengers of truth, that they are not destroyed; and when we go out to give the light with the special protection and power of God with us, we may stand against the power of Satan. Another feature: That is, the ones who have gone out in this work have obtained power. There is no question about that. Now no one can go out with the message, to meet that power which springs up from beneath, unless they have received the new light and life and power which has descended from on high, and taken possession of God's people who are not dead, as many now are, in trespasses and sins. I say, we might just as well look the matter right in the face, and do as the disciples of old did, tarry till we are imbued with power from on high. It is no use to go this way any longer, and my advice is most solemnly to every one who cannot go out now imbued with power from on high and bear this light from heaven, and to do the work that God has to be done now, stay at home.

Now I know that this is very severe. But I tell you, brethren, something must come to us, something must take hold of us; we cannot linger any longer or go on in a careless, easy-going manner. We cannot come to this assembly, this institute and Conference and go day after day in an easy-going manner. It is time for every one to be trembling in earnest for his own soul's salvation. Now just see what the instruction is; it was given and printed ten years ago. "We should pray as earnestly for the descent of the Holy Spirit as the disciples prayed on the day of Pentecost." Note what constituted prayer on that day of Pentecost. "It required all that time to bring them to an understanding of what it meant to offer effectual prayer, drawing nearer and nearer to God, confessing their sins, humbling their hearts before

God, and by faith beholding Jesus, and becoming changed into his image." Now I do not think that his great blessing will come to you and me individually, except we listen to this instruction. There is an individual work for every one of us to do in connection with this gathering, and that means solemn heart-searching before God, taking his word and repenting, that we may receive this power.

Now, to my mind, it does not mean that we can come here and go on as usual: get up in the morning, after breakfast have a social chat, come to this service and listen to it, talk and visit, come down at 2:30 and hear some more, and at 7:00 come and hear more; and come back and do the same thing again the next day. I tell you that will not bring it. It will not do it.

God is sending a special call to his people at this time. It is: Be zealous and repent, "or else I will come unto thee quickly, and will remove thy candlestick out of his place." Now, that is the simple situation that faces you and me to-night. The question is, What are we to do about it? What are you and I going to do about it, right here, now, at this Conference? That is the practical question, and the whole purpose of this instruction is to bring us face to face with that question. Again I say, What are we going to do about it?

We do not need new instruction so much as we do to act on the instruction that has already been given. I enjoy the seasons of coming together, and of listening to these instructions, and the explanation of God's word. This I enjoy very much. But I tell you, we might come and go here, week in and week out, year in and year out, and yet not meet the mind of God concerning this time. Take this word:-

"O, how we need the divine presence! For the baptism of the Holy Spirit, every worker should be breathing out his prayers to God. Companies should be gathered together to call upon God, for special help, for heavenly wisdom, that the people of God may know how to plan and devise and execute the work. Especially should men pray that the Lord will choose his agents, and baptize his missionaries with the Holy Spirit." - Special Testimony, No. 2, page 19.

Now here is the simple statement of it. At this time we expect to select men for various fields of labor, to send them out to the ends of the earth, to carry what? To carry the "loud cry" of the "third angel's message." It is no use for them to go, unless they have a message with the power of God's Spirit to go with them. The word is, that God's people should be meeting together in companies, calling upon him for special help, power, for the outpouring of his Spirit, as the disciples did on the day of Pentecost. Are we doing it? How long has this instruction been given us? It has been over six months (July 15, 1892), and I would like to know how many have taken this and acted upon it who are now at this Conference. I say it is no use trying to get ourselves into the notion that we may call upon God for his Holy Spirit while we neglect the plain instruction given as to how to prepare for it.

Let us look this right in the face. This is not a mere sentiment nor feeling; God wants to do this work right here and now, and he has sent us his instruction in every particular to tell us just how we may prepare for the outpouring of his Spirit. We [68] do not need so much new instruction given us as we do to act upon the instruction that we already have. I say it is time for us to begin now on these things. There is not a day to lose. Companies should be meeting together. We have not an hour to spend in visiting. God has not given us these privileges to use in that way. He has called us here together for a special thing, and he wants to bestow his Holy Spirit upon this people, as he did upon the disciples; and as it began at Jerusalem first, so he wants Battle Creek to receive the outpouring of his Spirit during the Institute and the Conference. And it is for you and me to say whether it shall be so or not. That is the plain statement of the case, and the lesson that I want to enforce. And it is a fact that because known sins are cherished by you and me that the power of

God's Spirit cannot come upon this people. God is calling upon us to confess those sins and to yield up these sinful desires, that he may remove them from us, even though it is like tearing the right hand from us. This is the experience that God is waiting for us to have.

Heb.10:26,27, "For if we sin wilfully after that we have received the knowledge of the truth, there remaineth no more sacrifice for sins, but a certain fearful looking for of judgment and fiery indignation, which shall devour the adversaries." Dr. Young translated it, "For if we sin wilfully, after that we have received the full knowledge of the truth." If we sin wilfully, then comes this experience.

Let us see how this compares with the testimony dated Aug. 20, 1892:-
"My brethren, we are living in a most solemn period of this earth's history. There is never a time to sin; it is always perilous to continue in transgression; but in a special sense is this true at the present time. We are now upon the very borders of the eternal world, and stand in a more solemn relation to time and to eternity than ever before." - Special Testimony, p.6.

While we stand here in the blaze of the light of the Spirit that God is sending us, it is a heinous thing in his sight to indulge in known sin, and even more so than before, because of the opportunity and the light that he is giving us. Again:-

"Now let every person search his own heart, and plead for the bright beams of the Sun of righteousness to expel all spiritual darkness and cleanse from defilement. 'If we confess our sins, he is faithful and just to forgive us our sins, and to cleanse us from all unrighteousness.'"

Well, it is simply a question of time, and, although I had a great deal more to present, I might as well stop here. But brethren, think about these things, pray about these things, let us do some serious, solemn work before God.

Made in the USA
Charleston, SC
18 February 2017